Grade 3

Scholastic Success With Maps

Contents

W9-DFT-548

Map Basics 2
Understanding Directions 4
The World on a Globe 6
Intermediate Directions 8
Using a Map Grid 10
Understanding Distance 12
Learning About Scale 14
Using a Map Scale 16
Comparing Maps 18
The United States 20
North America 22
South America 24
Landforms 26
Using a Landform Map 28
A Resource Map 30
A Rainfall Map 32
A History Map 34
A Tourist Map 36
A City Map 38
A Transit Map 40
Map Review 1 42
Map Review 2 43
Thinking About Maps 44
Glossary 45
Answers 47

BY LINDA WARD BEECH

SCHOLASTIC
PROFESSIONAL BOOKS

Map Basics

A map is a drawing of a place from above. A map can show all of Earth or just a small part of it. The map on this page shows a community.

Helpful Hint

Sometimes a map key is called a legend.

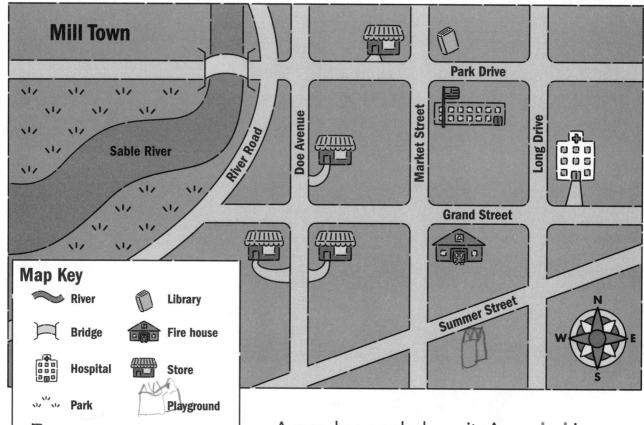

Mill Town

Park Drive

Sable River

River Road

Doe Avenue

Market Street

Long Drive

Grand Street

Summer Street

Map Key

- ∿ River
- 📖 Library
- ⌓ Bridge
- 🏠 Fire house
- 🏥 Hospital
- 🏪 Store
- ⋏⋏ Park
- 🛍 Playground
- 🏫 School

A map has symbols on it. A **symbol** is a drawing that stands for something real. A symbol can also be a color or a pattern. To learn what a map's symbols stand for, check the **map key**. The map key tells what each symbol means.

Use the map and map key to answer these questions.

1. What is the name of this community? _____

2. What does the symbol [hospital symbol] stand for? _____

3. What is the symbol for a park? _____

4. What body of water runs through the park? _____

5. How do you get across the river? _____

6. On what street are most of the stores? _____

7. Name three buildings you would see if you walked along Market Street. _____

_____

_____

8. On what street is the hospital? _____

9. Mill Town needs a new playground. Create your own symbol in the space at right and then draw it on the map and in the key.

Understanding Directions

This picture shows a **globe**.
A globe is a model of Earth.
A globe is the same shape as
Earth but much smaller.

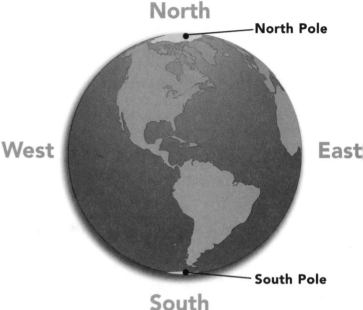

North

North Pole

West

East

South Pole

South

Read the labels on the globe.
The North and South poles help you
tell directions. North is toward the
North Pole. South is toward the
South Pole. When you face north,
east is to your right. West is to your left.

A compass rose is a symbol that
shows the four main directions on a map.
On a compass rose the letters **N**, **S**, **E**,
and **W** stand for the four directions.

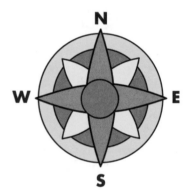

N

W

E

S

Complete these sentences.

1. The most northern place on the globe is the _____ .

2. The _____ is the most southern place on a globe.

3. On a compass rose, the letter W stands for _____ .

4. The direction East is sometimes written as _____ on a compass rose.

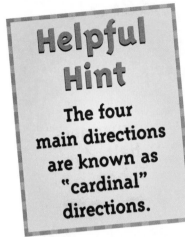

Helpful Hint

The four main directions are known as "cardinal" directions.

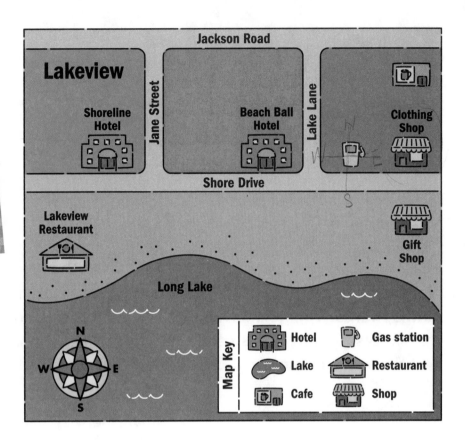

This map shows Lakeview. Use the compass rose to help answer these questions.

1. Is the lake on the north or south side of Lakeview?

_____

2. In which direction are the hotels from the lake?

_____

3. In which direction is the gift shop from the restaurant?

_____

4. Can you go north on Jackson Road? _____

5. What building is east of the gas station? _____

Word Search

Find and circle the four main directions.

R	E	A	S	T
H	T	R	O	N
L	S	Q	U	Z
O	E	N	T	Y
P	W	Y	H	L

The World on a Globe

Helpful Hint

"Hemi" means half. A "hemisphere" is half of a sphere.

A globe shows all of Earth. You can see Earth's continents and oceans on a globe.

The **equator** is an imaginary line that circles the globe halfway between the North and South poles. The equator divides Earth into two halves called **hemispheres**. The northern half is the Northern Hemisphere. What do you think the southern half is called? Earth can also be divided into Western and Eastern Hemispheres. Study the hemispheres on the globes.

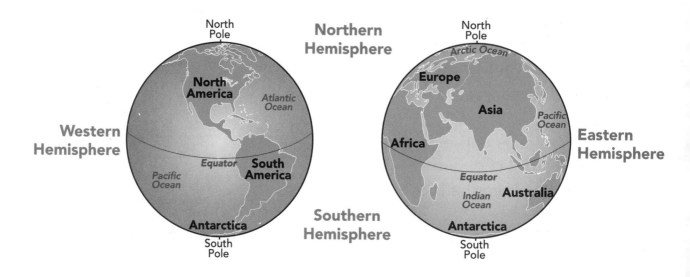

1. Does the equator run through North America? _____

2. What are the seven continents? _____

3. What are the four oceans? _____

4. In what hemispheres is most of South America? _____

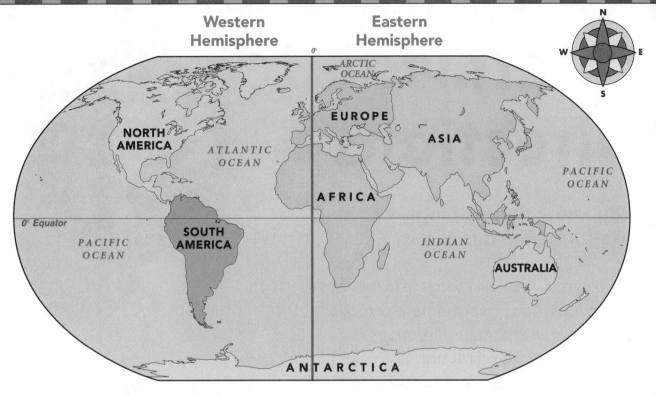

A globe is the best way to show what Earth looks like. However, globes are not so easy to carry around. So people use flat maps to represent Earth, too. Study the globes and map, then answer the questions.

1. Is Asia in the Eastern or Western Hemisphere? _____

2. What ocean is entirely north of the equator? _____

3. On the map, is east to the right or to the left? _____

4. The North Pole is at the _____ of the globe.

5. The area south of the
   equator is called the Southern _____ .

Code Word

Fill in the blanks with the first letter of the answers for questions 1-5 to figure out the secret code word.

_____	_____	_____	_____	_____
1.	2.	3.	4.	5.

Intermediate Directions

You know that a compass rose has four main directions.

A compass rose can show **intermediate directions**, too. Intermediate directions are between the main directions. For example, the direction between north and west is northwest. Letters sometimes stand for the intermediate directions on a compass rose. For example, NE stands for northeast.

Answer these questions.

1. What direction is between south and east?_____

2. What direction is between north and east?_____

3. What direction is opposite of northwest?_____

4. What do the letters NW stand for on a compass rose? _____

5. What letters stand for southwest? _____

This map shows an **intersection**.
An intersection is where two roads cross.
Find the bank on the map. It is east of Water Street and north of Central Avenue. So the bank is on the northeast corner of the intersection.

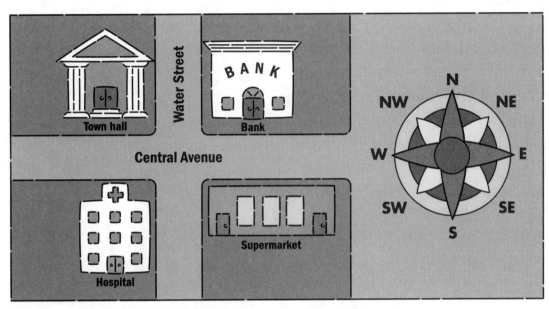

Color each compass rose to show the correct direction.

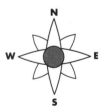 1. In what direction is the town hall from the hospital?

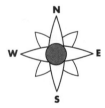 2. On which corner is the supermarket?

3. On which corner is the hospital?

4. You ran out of money at the supermarket. In which direction do you go to get more?

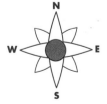 5. In which direction would you go from the supermarket to the town hall?

Using a Map Grid

Some maps have a **grid** on them.

A grid is a pattern of lines that cross to form squares.
Each square on a grid has a letter and a number.
Find the letter A at the left side of the map.
Then locate the number 1 along the top of the map.
The first square in the top row is A1. Now find A2.

Helpful Hint

A grid makes it easier to pinpoint places on a map.

Use the map to answer these questions.

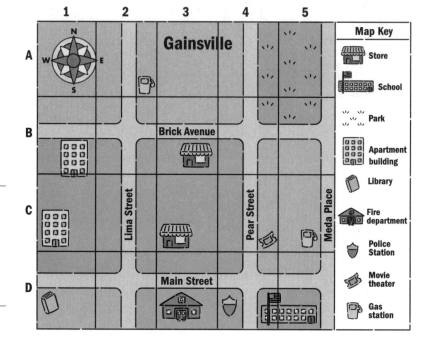

1. What building is in D1?

   _____

2. In which square is the police station?

   _____

3. Name all the squares that Lima Street runs through.

   _____

4. In which squares is the school located? _____

5. Can you buy gas in C5? _____

Sometimes a map has letters and numbers along the side and top, but no grid lines. Then you must imagine where the lines go. For example, look in B1 and C1 to find the apartment buildings in Gainsville.

Use the map to answer these questions.

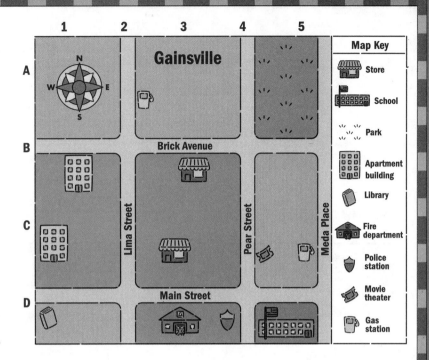

1. What building is in D3? _____

2. Find the park in A4. In what other square is the park? _____

3. What squares does Meda Place run through? _____

4. What is in C3? _____

5. Find C4. What can you do there? _____

My Tour of Gainsville

Pretend you are giving a new friend a tour of Gainsville. You visit the squares in this order: C1, D1, C3, A4, C4. Write a list describing the places you will visit.

1. _____
2. _____
3. _____
4. _____
5. _____

Understanding Distance

A map can show where places are in relation to one another.

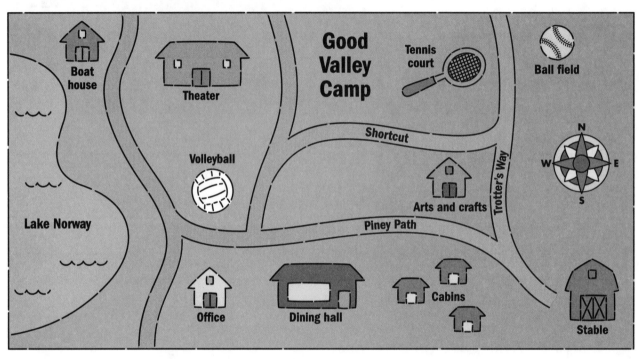

Use the map to answer these questions.

1. What is the nearest building to the lake? _____

2. What building is farthest from the theater? _____

3. What is the nearest building to the west of the dining hall? _____

4. What is the nearest building to the north of the cabins? _____

5. Is the volleyball court nearer
   the ball field or the tennis court? _____

A map can show **distance**, or how far it is from one place to another. This map has lines between the towns. The number on each line tells how many miles it is from one town to another. For example, it is 20 miles from Dover to Clark City.

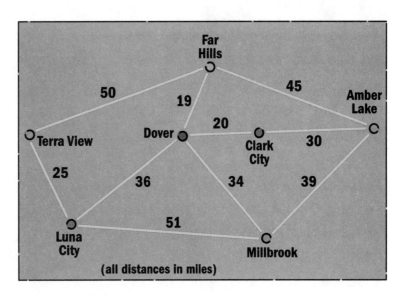

Far
Hills

50   19   45   Amber
                        Lake

20
Terra View   Dover   30
                Clark
                City
25

36   34   39

51

Luna
City   Millbrook

(all distances in miles)

1. How far is it from Terra View to Luna City? _____

2. How many miles is Amber Lake from Far Hills? _____

3. Will it take longer to drive from Millbrook to Luna City or from Millbrook to Dover? _____

4. What is the shortest way from Clark City to Terra View? _____

   How many miles would it be? _____

5. What is the closest town to Dover? _____

Distance is one thing that you need to know when you plan a trip. Other things make a difference, too. For example, it takes longer to drive over a mountain than it does to cross a plain. Draw a picture of something else that could make a car trip take longer.

Learning About Scale

A map is not the same size as the place it shows. It is much smaller. Places on a map are inches or less apart.

To show distance on a map, mapmakers use a **scale**.

A scale is a kind of ruler that helps you measure distance on a map. Look at the scale on this map. It shows that one inch equals ten feet. That means one inch on the map stands for ten feet of the real place.

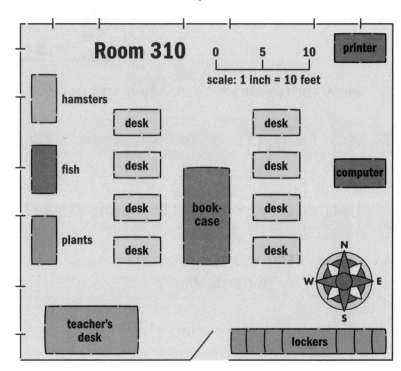

Room 310

scale: 1 inch = 10 feet

hamsters

fish

plants

teacher's desk

desk desk desk desk

book-case

desk desk desk desk

printer

computer

lockers

Use a ruler to measure the distances on the map.

1. How many feet is the classroom from the east side to the west side? _____

2. How far is the bookcase from the door? _____

3. How far is the teacher's desk from the lockers? _____

4. How far are the fish from the computer? _____

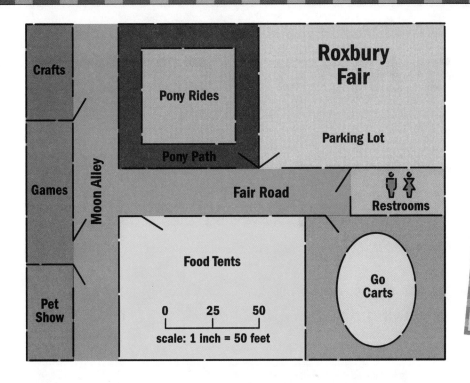

Roxbury Fair

Crafts

Pony Rides

Pony Path

Games

Moon Alley

Fair Road

Parking Lot

Restrooms

Food Tents

0   25   50

scale: 1 inch = 50 feet

Go Carts

Pet Show

Helpful Hint

When you use a map scale, you may need to add, subtract, or multiply.

Always check the map scale to find the distance it represents. Use a ruler to help you answer these questions.

1. How long is Fair Road? _____

2. How wide is the parking lot? _____

3. About how many feet is it from
    the games entrance to the crafts entrance? _____

4. How far is it from the pet show
    entrance to the gate of the go carts? _____

5. If a pony goes once around the
    pony path, how far does it go? _____

Using a Map Scale

A map scale often looks like this:

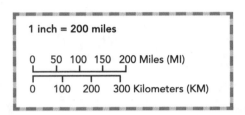

1 inch = 200 miles

```
0    50  100  150   200 Miles (MI)
|----|----|----|----|
0    100    200    300 Kilometers (KM)
```

The MI on the scale stands for miles, and the KM stands for kilometers. Kilometers are a way of measuring distance in the Metric System.

Helpful Hint

When measuring distance on a map, always line up the end of the ruler with the "zero" on the map scale.

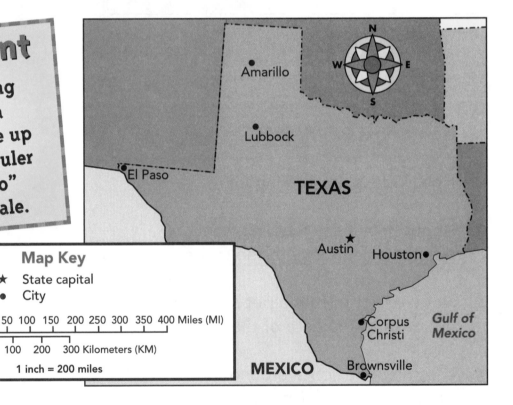

Map Key

★ State capital
● City

```
0  50 100 150 200 250 300 350 400 Miles (MI)
|--|--|--|--|--|--|--|--|
0   100   200   300 Kilometers (KM)
```
1 inch = 200 miles

Use the map scale to answer these questions.

1. From Houston to Austin it is about _____ miles.

2. Corpus Christi is about _____ miles from Houston.

3. Lubbock is about _____ miles from El Paso.

4. Is a kilometer longer or shorter than a mile? _____

5. It is a little less than 450
   miles from Austin to _____ .

6. Are Brownsville and Corpus Christi
   more or less than 150 miles apart? _____

7. Corpus Christi and Austin are about
   300 _____ apart.

8. From the capital of Texas to El Paso it is about _____
   miles.

9. From its most northern part to its most
   southern part, Texas is about _____ miles long.

10. The widest part of Texas is about 1,200 _____ across.

Helpful Hint

If you don't have a ruler, lay the edge of a piece of paper along the map scale. Mark the paper, then use it to measure distances on the map.

Word Search

Find and circle four Texas cities.

N	O	R	A	O	Z	X	L	Y
A	S	L	U	B	B	O	C	K
M	A	V	S	K	Y	E	G	J
S	P	T	T	L	P	S	U	W
O	L	L	I	R	A	M	A	O
T	E	Q	N	H	O	X	F	B

Comparing Maps

Maps can show places of different sizes.

Look at the maps on these pages. One map shows a state. One map shows a country, and the third map shows a continent.

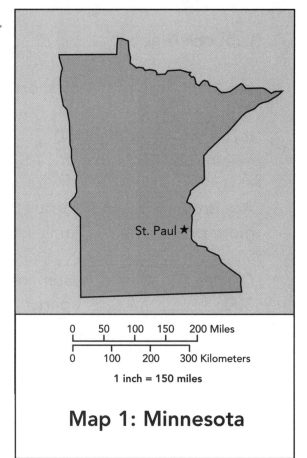

Helpful Hint

Even on maps with different scales, the distance between two places is always the same.

Map 1: Minnesota

Use the maps to answer these questions.

1. What state does Map 1 show? _____

2. What does one inch stand for on the scale for Map 1? _____

3. The abbreviation for this state is MN.
   Find it on Map 2. Does Map 1 or Map 2 cover a larger area? _____

4. What does one inch stand for on Map 2? _____

5. About how many miles is it from the coast
   of California (CA) to the coast of Virginia (VA)? _____

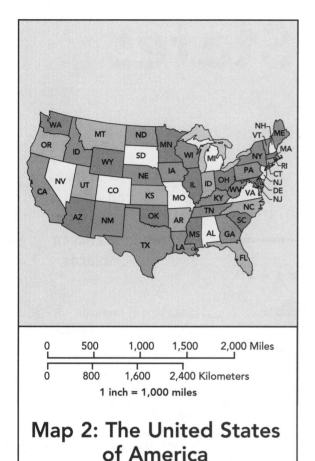

0   500   1,000   1,500   2,000 Miles

0   800   1,600   2,400 Kilometers

1 inch = 1,000 miles

Map 2: The United States of America

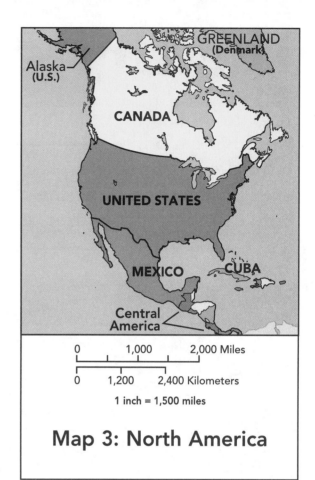

0   1,000   2,000 Miles

0   1,200   2,400 Kilometers

1 inch = 1,500 miles

Map 3: North America

6. What does one inch stand for on Map 3? _____

7. What does Map 3 show? _____

8. Which of the maps shows the largest area? _____

9. Which of the maps shows the smallest area? _____

10. On Map 3, draw a box that shows the area shown on Map 2. Then draw another box on the map to show the area on Map 1.

The United States

You are looking at the United States.
Find this symbol —————— on the map.
A **border** shows where places begin and
end. Borders can show the dividing lines
between states, countries, and other places.

Rivers
and lakes
can also form
borders
between
places.

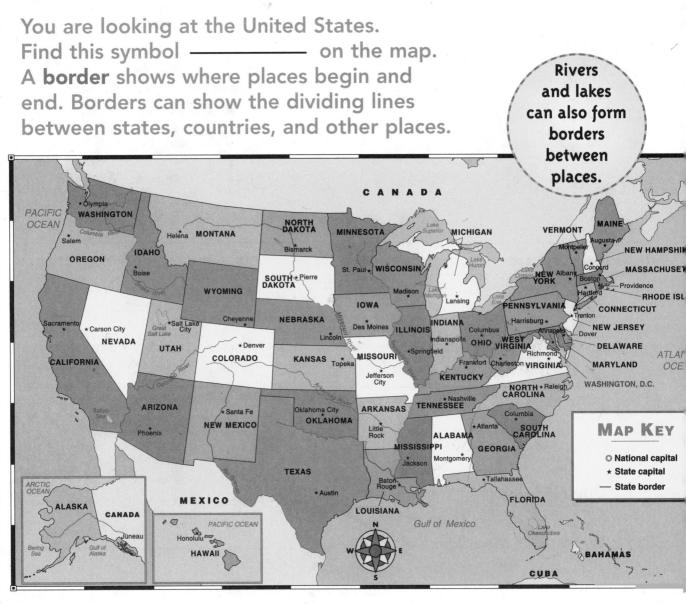

Read the map, then answer these questions.

1. Find Alabama. What state shares
   a border with it on the west? _____

2. Find Colorado. What states share
   a border with it on the east? _____

3. What lake forms part of the northwest border of Pennsylvania?

_____

4. What river forms the western border of Tennessee?

_____

Helpful Hint

Two states do not touch any other states. Both of these states are far from the rest of the country. These states are shown in small boxes called inset maps.

5. Which states are shown in the inset maps? _____

6. What is the capital of Alaska? _____

7. Hawaii is in the Pacific Ocean. In which direction is it from California? _____

"Speedy Map Planner"

Imagine that you are taking a trip from the Atlantic Ocean to the Pacific Ocean. Plan a route that passes through the fewest number of states possible. Can you do it in less than eight states? Write the states on the chart.

1. _____	5. _____
2. _____	6. _____
3. _____	7. _____
4. _____	8. _____

North America

The United States is on the continent of North America.

Two countries, Canada and Mexico, share borders with the United States. North America also includes Greenland, the countries of Central America, and many islands.

Helpful Hint

One state, Hawaii, is not part of North America.

Use the map to answer these questions about North America.

1. In which direction is Mexico from the United States? _____

2. Name two other countries that share a border with Mexico. _____

3. What country shares a border on the north with the United States? _____

4. What state is on the northwest part of North America? _____

5. What oceans border the east and west coasts of North America? _____

6. What ocean is north of this continent? _____

7. What is the capital of Canada? _____

8. What river forms part of the border between the U.S. and Mexico? _____

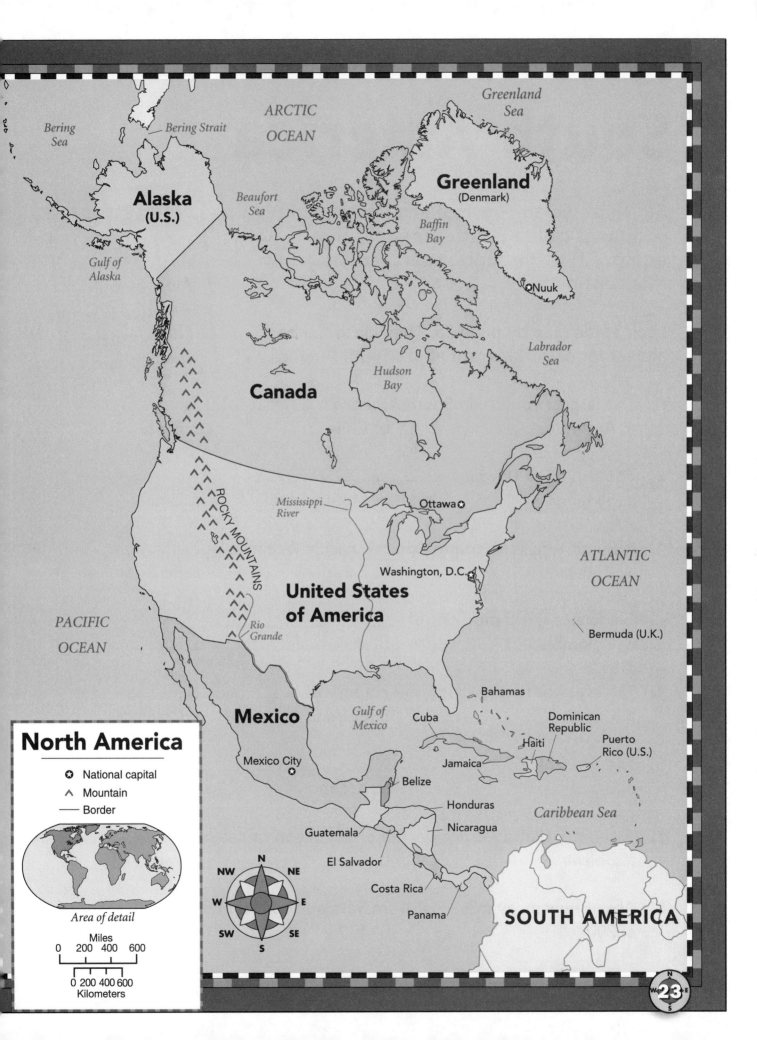

ARCTIC OCEAN

Greenland Sea

Bering Sea

Bering Strait

Alaska (U.S.)

Beaufort Sea

Greenland
(Denmark)

Baffin Bay

Gulf of Alaska

Nuuk

Labrador Sea

Hudson Bay

Canada

ROCKY MOUNTAINS

Mississippi River

Ottawa ✪

ATLANTIC OCEAN

PACIFIC OCEAN

Rio Grande

United States of America

Washington, D.C.

Bermuda (U.K.)

Mexico

Gulf of Mexico

Bahamas

Cuba

Dominican Republic

Haiti

Puerto Rico (U.S.)

Mexico City ✪

Jamaica

Belize

Honduras

Guatemala

Nicaragua

Caribbean Sea

El Salvador

Costa Rica

Panama

SOUTH AMERICA

North America

✪ National capital
∧ Mountain
— Border

Area of detail

Miles
0 200 400 600

0 200 400 600
Kilometers

N
NW   NE
W   E
SW   SE
S

South America

South of North America lies another big continent called South America. The equator runs through several countries of this continent.

Look at the map on page 25. Then circle the best answer for each statement about South America.

Helpful Hint
Most of South America is in the Southern Hemisphere.

1. The largest country in South America is _____ .
   a. Argentina   b. Chile   c. Brazil

2. The capital of Uruguay is _____ .
   a. Santiago   b. Montevideo   c. Lima

3. A South American country on the Pacific Ocean is _____ .
   a. Guyana   b. Paraguay   c. Ecuador

4. Caracas is the capital city of _____ .
   a. Colombia   b. Venezuela   c. Suriname

5. The equator runs through the country of _____ .
   a. Chile   b. Guyana   c. Colombia

6. The Amazon River flows across _____ .
   a. Brazil   b. Argentina   c. Paraguay

7. A country that does not border on an ocean or sea is _____ .
   a. Bolivia   b. Peru   c. Venezuela

8. About how many miles is it from Santiago to Montevideo? _____ .
   a. 200   b. 400   c. 900

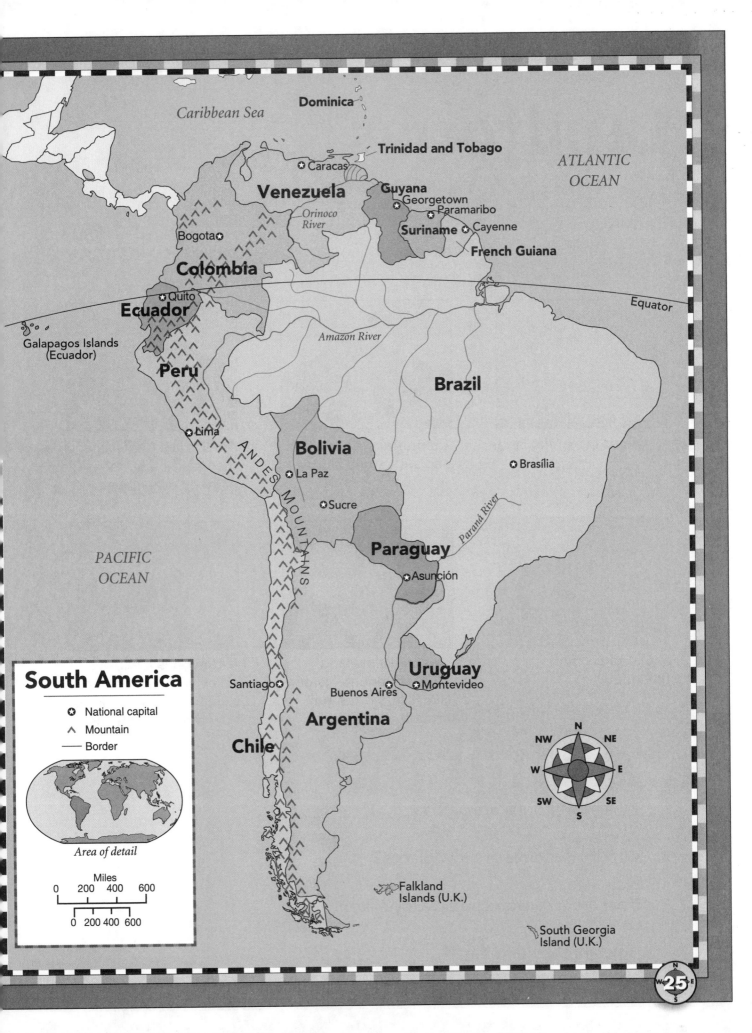

Caribbean Sea

Dominica

Trinidad and Tobago

ATLANTIC
OCEAN

Caracas
Venezuela
Orinoco
River

Guyana
Georgetown
Paramaribo
Suriname
Cayenne
French Guiana

Bogota

Colombia

Quito
Ecuador

Equator

Galapagos Islands
(Ecuador)

Amazon River

Peru

Brazil

Lima

ANDES MOUNTAINS

Bolivia

La Paz

Brasília

Sucre

Paraná River

PACIFIC
OCEAN

Paraguay

Asunción

Uruguay

Santiago

Buenos Aires

Montevideo

Argentina

Chile

Falkland
Islands (U.K.)

South Georgia
Island (U.K.)

South America

⊛ National capital

∧ Mountain

— Border

Area of detail

Miles

0   200 400   600

0   200 400 600

N
NW   NE
W   E
SW   SE
S

25

Landforms

Maps are usually drawn on paper, so the land looks flat. But you know that Earth's land is not always flat. In fact, the land takes many shapes called **landforms**. The pictures show some important landforms.

A **plain** is open, flat land.

A **mountain** is very high land with steep slopes.

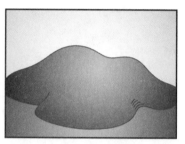

A **hill** is land that is higher than a plain but not as high or steep as a mountain.

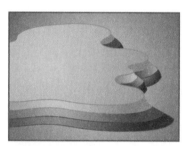

A **plateau** is high, flat land.

A **valley** is low land between mountains or hills. Rivers often run through a valley.

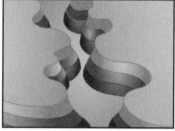

A **canyon** is a narrow valley with high, steep sides. Rivers sometimes flow through canyons, too.

Use the pictures to answer these questions.

1. Which landforms are high land? _____

2. Which landforms are low places? _____

3. How are a canyon and a valley alike? _____

   How are they different? _____

More than half of Earth is covered with water.

You have learned about some of these bodies of water such as oceans, rivers, and lakes. The picture shows some other bodies of water and some other landforms.

Use the maps to help answer the questions.

A **gulf** is part of an ocean or sea. A gulf is partly surrounded by land.

A **bay** is like a gulf but smaller.

An **island** is land that is completely surrounded by water.

A **peninsula** is an "almost island." It is land that is surrounded by water on all but one side.

1. Why might a bay be a good place to keep a boat? _____

2. How is a bay like a gulf? _____

3. Find Florida on the map on page 20. What landform is Florida? _____

4. How is a peninsula different from an island? _____

5. In what way are a lake and an island similar? _____

Using a Landform Map

Helpful Hint

A landform map is sometimes called a relief map.

This is a landform map of Arkansas.

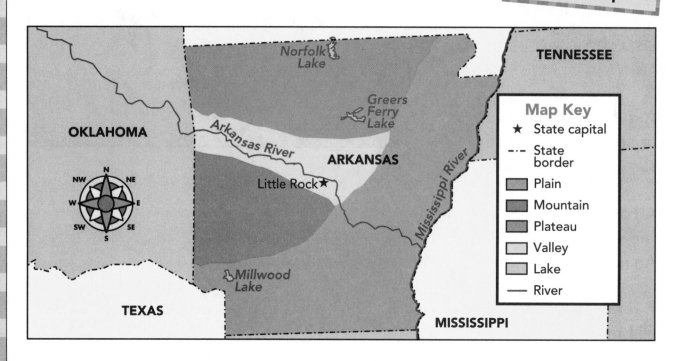

Study the map, then answer these questions.

1. What does the symbol [ ] stand for? _____

2. What is the symbol for mountains? _____

3. What landform covers most of the northern part of the state? _____

4. What body of water forms the eastern border of Arkansas? _____

5. In which parts of the state would you find plains? _____

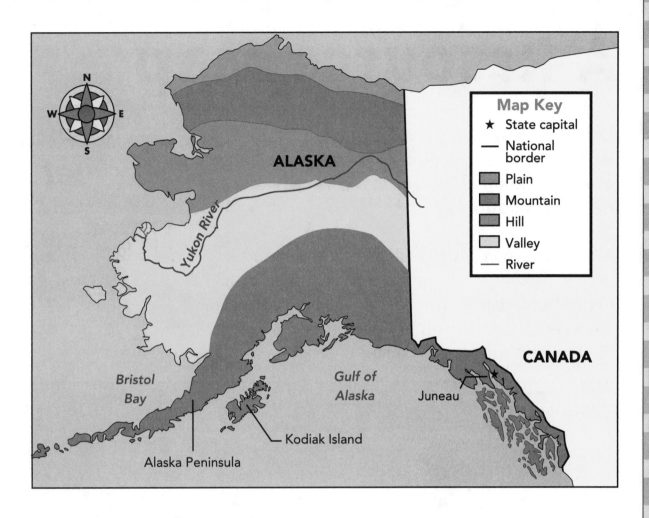

This map shows the landforms of Alaska.
Study the map, then answer these questions.

1. In which part of Alaska are there plains? _____

2. Name a large island off the
   southern part of the state. _____

3. What is the land that extends from the
   southwest part of the state called? _____

4. On what kind of land is Alaska's capital? _____

5. What river runs across the state? _____

A Resource Map

Do you know what coal is? It's a kind of rock that is burned to make heat and energy. Coal is just one of Pennsylvania's **natural resources**.

A natural resource is something found in nature that people use. Air, water, plants, soil, and minerals are all natural resources. A map can show where natural resources are located. The map on this page shows where some of Pennsylvania's mineral resources are found.

Helpful Hint

A mineral is a resource that is found in the ground.

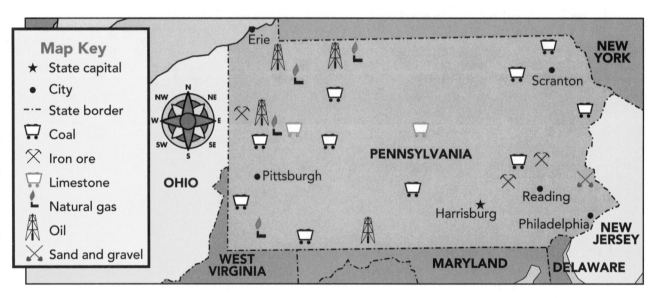

Answer these questions.

1. How are natural resources helpful to people? _____

_____

2. What are some ways people use sand and gravel? _____

3. Why is a flame a good symbol for natural gas? _____

Much of Pennsylvania's coal is burned to make electricity.

Write **TRUE** or **FALSE** on the line.
Use the map on page 30 to help you.

_____ 1. Most of Pennsylvania's oil is in the northwest part of the state.

_____ 2. Sand and gravel are found in the east.

_____ 3. Most of the state's iron ore is in the north.

_____ 4. Pennsylvania has no natural gas.

_____ 5. Pennsylvania has more coal than oil.

_____ 6. The symbol ⚒ stands for oil.

An Amazing Journey

Use this Pennsylvania maze to get from Philadelphia to the oil field in the northwest.

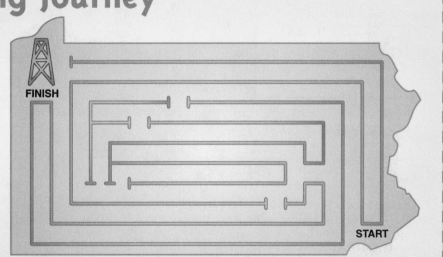

A Rainfall Map

Water is the most important natural resource. Plants, animals, and people all need water. Water falls to Earth as rain, snow, sleet, and hail.

This map is called a rainfall map. It shows how much water falls in the different parts of Maine during one year.

Helpful Hint

Another word for rainfall is precipitation.

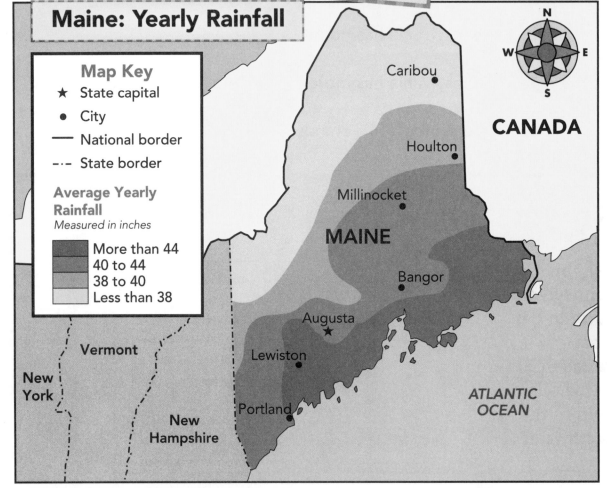

Maine: Yearly Rainfall

Map Key
- ★ State capital
- ● City
- — National border
- -·- State border

Average Yearly Rainfall
Measured in inches
- More than 44
- 40 to 44
- 38 to 40
- Less than 38

Caribou

CANADA

Houlton

Millinocket

MAINE

Bangor

Augusta

Lewiston

Vermont

New York

New Hampshire

Portland

ATLANTIC OCEAN

People use water to drink and to bathe. Water is also important for growing crops, washing things, and running machines.

Use the map to answer these questions.

1. This symbol ▭ stands for ____________________ inches.

2. The least amount of rain in Maine falls in the ____________________ parts of the state.

3. Bangor gets about ____________________ inches of rain a year.

4. A city in Maine that gets 38 to 40 inches of rain a year is ____________.

5. The city on this map that gets the most rain is ____________________.

6. The rainfall in Houlton is ____________________ than in Caribou.

7. You can guess that the part of Canada near the northwest part of Maine gets ____________ inches of rain a year.

Connect the words to the correct symbols.

1. rain **2. snow** **3. sleet** **4. hail**

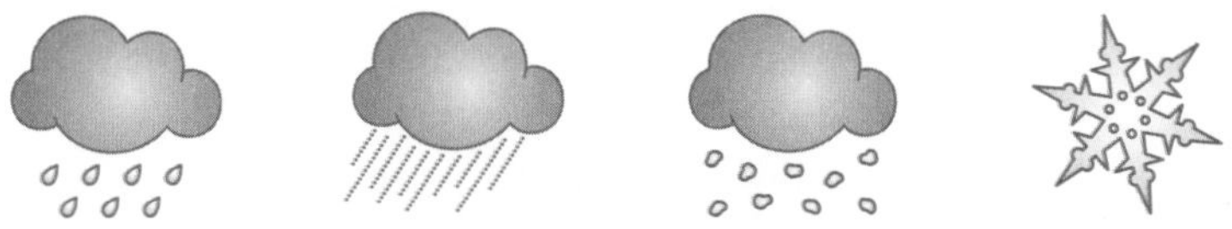

A History Map

You can learn about the past from a map. The map on this page shows the Oregon Trail. This was a **route** that pioneers followed when they traveled west in the 1840s. A route is a way to go from one place to another.

In the 1840s people did not have airplanes or cars. They traveled in covered wagons pulled by oxen. Some pioneers rode on horses or walked alongside the wagons. Most pioneers met in Independence, Missouri, and formed groups. The groups traveled together in wagon trains.

Oregon Trail

PACIFIC OCEAN

CANADA

WASHINGTON

Columbia River

UNITED STATES

Portland

Missouri River

MINNESOTA

Oregon City

MONTANA

NORTH DAKOTA

OREGON

IDAHO

Three Island Crossing

ROCKY

WYOMING

SOUTH DAKOTA

Snake River

Independence Rock

NEVADA

Fort Laramie

NEBRASKA

IOWA

Great Salt Lake

Fort Bridger

MOUNTAINS

Platte River

N
W   E
S

Map Key

- City or town
- Oregon Trail
- River
- Mountain

UTAH

COLORADO

KANSAS

Independence

CALIFORNIA

ARIZONA

NEW MEXICO

TEXAS

OKLAHOMA

Use the map to answer these questions.

1. In what direction did the trail go
   from Independence to Portland? _____

2. What river flows by Independence? _____

3. After Independence, what was the
   first town along the trail? _____

4. What mountains did the Oregon Trail cross? _____

5. Find Three Island Crossing. On what river is it? _____

6. Why do you think the Oregon Trail
   does not follow a straight line? _____

7. The wagon trains left Independence in May for
   the five-month trip. Why do you think it was
   important to start then? _____

Helpful Hint

In 1840 most of the land west of the Mississippi River was not yet divided into states.

Word Scramble

Below are the names of four present-day states that the Oregon trail passed through. Can you figure out what they are?

NOROGE	AIHDO	ARBNAKSE	ANSSKA
_____	_____	_____	_____

A Tourist Map

A tourist is someone who travels for fun.

If you have ever been a tourist, you know that it is handy to have a map of the place you are visiting. A **tourist map** shows a place of interest and highlights the special things to see and do there.

Saguaro West is in the Sonoran Desert. This land was set aside as a park because of the special plants and animals that live there.

This map shows a large park in Arizona called Saguaro West.

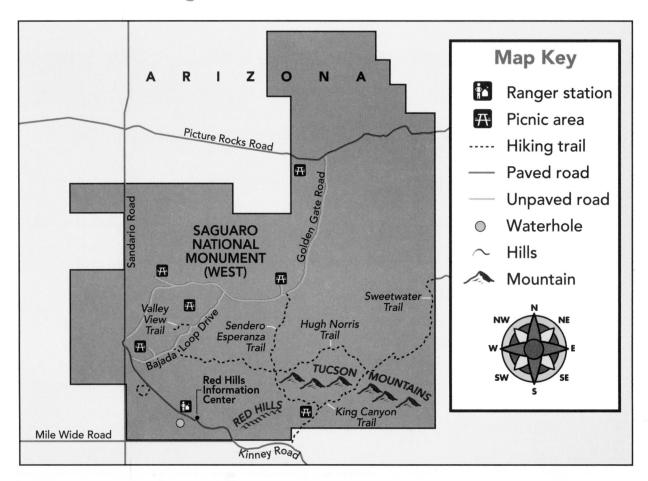

A R I Z O N A

Picture Rocks Road

Sandario Road

SAGUARO NATIONAL MONUMENT (WEST)

Golden Gate Road

Sweetwater Trail

Valley View Trail

Bajada Loop Drive

Sendero Esperanza Trail

Hugh Norris Trail

TUCSON MOUNTAINS

Red Hills Information Center

RED HILLS

King Canyon Trail

Mile Wide Road

Kinney Road

Map Key

👥 Ranger station

🅰 Picnic area

- - - - Hiking trail

—— Paved road

—— Unpaved road

⊙ Waterhole

∼ Hills

⛰ Mountain

NW N NE
W   E
SW S SE

Helpful Hint

Saguaro is the name of a large cactus.

Study the map, then answer these questions.

1. What does the symbol 🏕 mean? _____

2. In what part of the park is the Ranger Station? _____

3. From the Ranger Station, how would
   you drive to the northernmost picnic area? _____

   _____

4. What kind of plants would you expect to see in this park? _____

   _____

5. What does this symbol ⬤ mean? _____

   Why might animals come there? _____

6. What road cuts through the park on
   the west side going from north to south? _____

A City Map

Welcome to New York City!
Part of this city is on the island of
Manhattan. The map shows some of
the main streets in Manhattan. Use
the map to answer the questions.

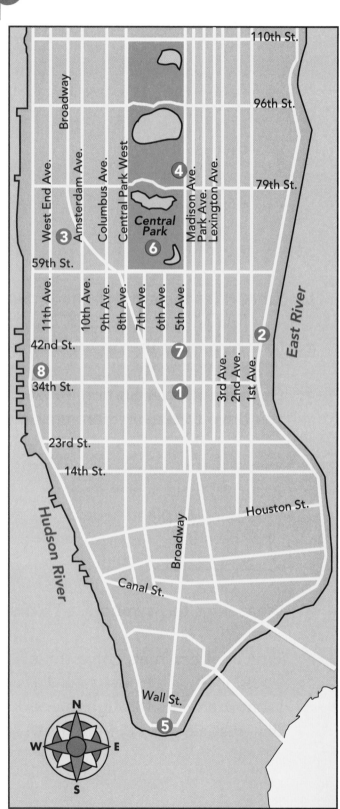

1. What river runs along the
    west side of Manhattan?

    _____

    Along the east side?

    _____

2. The direction the streets run is

    from _____ to _____ .

3. The avenues run from

    _____ to _____ .

4. One of the oldest streets is
    Wall Street. In which part of
    Manhattan is it?

    _____

Helpful Hint

As you move north in Manhattan, the numbers of the streets get higher.

Many of New York's streets form a grid pattern.

This grid makes it easier to find places in the city. For example, the Empire State Building is on the corner of Fifth Avenue and 34th Street. Use the map to answer the questions.

5. What street runs along the southern part of Central Park? _____

What avenues run along the east and west sides of the park? _____

6. Find the New York Public Library. On what corner is it found? _____

7. On which side of the city is the United Nations? _____

8. Find the Empire State Building. In which direction would you walk to get to the Javits Center? _____

9. Why do you think the streets of New York City are numbered?

_____

A Transit Map

How do you get to school? How do people in your family get to work?

In many communities people use public transportation. They take buses or trains to get from one part of the community to another. A **transit map** shows the route a bus or train takes.

Helpful Hint

San Francisco is located on a peninsula between San Francisco Bay and the Pacific Ocean.

The transit map on this page shows BART trains in San Francisco, California. BART stands for Bay Area Rapid Transit. The map shows the routes that BART trains take to connect San Francisco to communities around it.

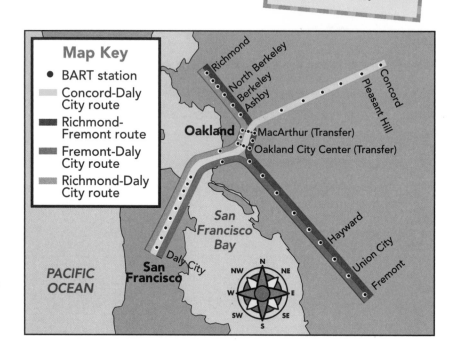

Use the map to answer these questions.

1. What does this symbol ▬▬▬ stand for on this map? _____

2. What color is the Richmond-Fremont Route? _____

3. On what line is the Pleasant Hill stop? _____

The BART lines come together and form a kind of X.

Find the Oakland City Center stop. Do you see the word "transfer" after it? At a transfer stop, passengers can change from one line to another.

4. Can you travel on the same train to
   get from Concord to Daly City? _____

5. What are the stops at the end of each BART line? _____

   _____

6. What is special about the MacArthur stop? _____

7. What BART line does not go into San Francisco? _____

8. In which direction do the BART lines
   go from Daly City to Oakland? _____

9. What body of water do three of the BART lines cross? _____

   _____

10. Without BART, how do you think people
    could get from Oakland to San Francisco? _____

Design a Symbol

BART is looking for a new symbol
to show transfer stations on its
map. Use this space to draw your
own symbol.

Map Review 1

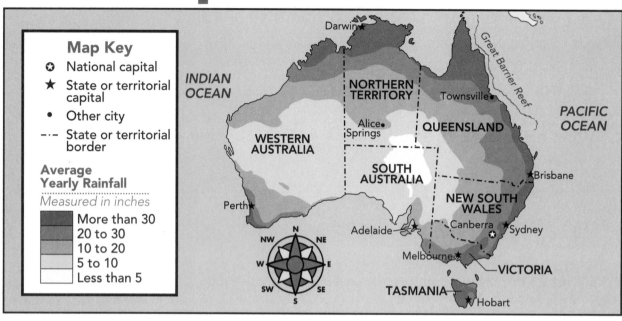

Map Key
- ✪ National capital
- ★ State or territorial capital
- • Other city
- -·- State or territorial border

Average Yearly Rainfall
Measured in inches
- More than 30
- 20 to 30
- 10 to 20
- 5 to 10
- Less than 5

INDIAN OCEAN

Darwin★

NORTHERN TERRITORY

Townsville•

PACIFIC OCEAN

Great Barrier Reef

Alice Springs•

QUEENSLAND

WESTERN AUSTRALIA

SOUTH AUSTRALIA

Perth★

Brisbane★

NEW SOUTH WALES

Adelaide★

Canberra✪ Sydney•

Melbourne★

VICTORIA

TASMANIA

Hobart★

NW N NE
W E
SW S SE

Use the map to answer the questions.

1. What does the symbol ☐ stand for? _____

2. Does Australia get more rain along the coasts or inland?

   _____

3. About how much rain a year does Alice Springs get?

   _____

4. Part of Australia is desert. About how much rain do you think this part of the country gets? _____

5. What is the national capital of Australia? _____

6. What oceans surround Australia? _____

7. On which part of the continent is New South Wales?

   _____

8. Check the words that are true for Australia:
   _____ continent
   _____ country
   _____ island

Map Review 2

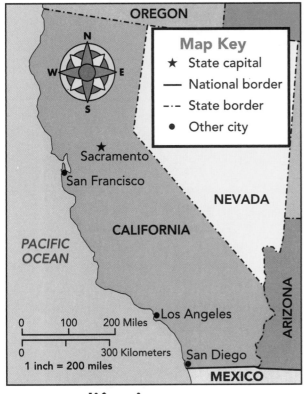

Map Key
★ State capital
— National border
-·-· State border
● Other city

Map 1: California

Map 2: Los Angeles

Use the maps to answer these questions.

1. Which map shows a larger place? _____

2. How many miles does one inch stand for on the map of California? _____

3. How many miles does one inch stand for on the map of Los Angeles? _____

4. What is the capital of California? _____

5. About how many miles is it from Sacramento to San Diego?

   _____

6. What body of water is to the west of California? _____

7. What states border California on the east? _____

   _____

8. What does this symbol ——— stand for? _____

Thinking About Maps

Across

2. a narrow valley with steep sides

4. "Southeast" is an _____ direction.

8. lines that cross to form squares on a map

9. water that is completely surrounded by land

10. The United States is located in the northern _____.

11. This symbol shows directions.

Down

1. a dividing line between states or countries

2. South America is a _____.

3. _____ helps you measure distance on a map.

5. Coal is a natural _____.

6. how far one place is from another

7. Hills and plateaus are kinds of _____.

Glossary

bay
A bay is part of an ocean or sea that is partly surrounded by land. A bay is smaller than a gulf.

border
A border shows where places begin and end. It is a dividing line between places.

canyon
A canyon is a narrow valley with high, steep sides.

compass rose
A compass rose is a symbol that shows the four main directions on a map.

distance
Distance is how far it is from one place to another.

equator
The equator is an imaginary line that circles the globe halfway between the North and South poles.

globe
A globe is a model of Earth.

grid
A grid is a pattern of lines that cross to form squares.

gulf
A gulf is part of an ocean or sea that is partly surrounded by land.

hemisphere
A hemisphere is a half of Earth. Earth can be divided into Northern and Southern hemispheres or Eastern and Western hemispheres.

inset map
An inset map is a small map in a box that is shown with a larger map.

intermediate directions
Intermediate directions are between the main directions. The direction between south and east is southeast.

intersection
An intersection is where two roads cross or intersect.

island
An island is land that is completely surrounded by water.

landform
A landform is the shape of land such as a mountain. A landform map is sometimes called a relief map.

map key
A map key is a list of symbols used on a map. A map key is also called a legend.

natural resource
A natural resource is something found in nature that people use.

peninsula
A peninsula is land that is surrounded by water on all but one side.

plateau
A plateau is high, flat land. It is sometimes called a tableland.

rainfall
Rainfall is water that falls to Earth in the form of rain, snow, sleet, and hail. Rainfall is also called precipitation.

route
A route is a way to go from one place to another.

scale
A scale is a kind of ruler that helps you measure distance on a map.

symbol
A symbol is a drawing that stands for something real. A symbol can also be a color or a pattern.

tourist map
A tourist map shows interesting places and high-lights things to see and do.

transit map
A transit map shows the route that a bus or train takes.

valley
A valley is low land that runs between mountains or hills.

Answers

PAGES 2–3:
1. Mill Town
2. hospital
3. grass
4. Sable River
5. bridge
6. Doe Avenue
7. fire house, school, library
8. Grand Street

PAGE 4:
1. North Pole
2. South Pole
3. west
4. E

PAGE 5:
1. south
2. north
3. east
4. no
5. clothing shop

PAGES 6:
1. no
2. North America, South America, Asia, Africa, Australia, Antarctica, Europe
3. Indian, Arctic, Pacific, Atlantic
4. Western and Southern

PAGE 7:
1. Eastern
2. Arctic
3. right
4. top
5. Hemisphere
Code word: Earth

PAGE 8:
1. southeast
2. northeast
3. southeast
4. northwest
5. SW

PAGE 9:
1. north
2. southeast
3. southwest
4. north
5. northwest

PAGE 10:
1. library
2. D4
3. A2, B2, C2, D2
4. D4, D5
5. yes

PAGE 11:
1. fire department
2. A5
3. A5, B5, C5, D5
4. store
5. go to the movies
My tour: apartment building; library; store; park; movie theater

PAGE 12:
1. boat house
2. stable
3. office
4. arts and crafts
5. tennis court

PAGE 13:
1. 25 miles
2. 45 miles
3. Luna City
4. Clark City to Dover to Luna City to Terra View; 81 miles
5. Far HIlls

PAGE 14:
1. 40 feet
2. 10 feet
3. 10 feet
4. 30 feet

PAGE 15:
1. 125 feet
2. 100 feet
3. 75 feet
4. about 150 feet
5. 200 feet

PAGES 16–17:
1. 150
2. 200
3. 300
4. shorter
5. Amarillo
6. less
7. kilometers
8. 500
9. 800
10. kilometers

PAGES 18–19:
1. Minnesota
2. 150 miles
3. Map 2
4. 1,000 miles
5. about 2,500
6. 1,500 miles
7. North America
8. more land is shown on Map 3
9. Map 1

PAGES 20–21:
1. Mississippi
2. Kansas and Nebraska
3. Lake Erie
4. Mississippi River
5. Alaska and Hawaii
6. Juneau
7. west
8. North Carolina, Tennessee, Arkansas, Oklahoma, New Mexico, Arizona, California

PAGE 22:
1. south
2. Belize, Guatemala
3. Canada
4. Alaska
5. Atlantic; Pacific
6. Arctic
7. Ottawa
8. Rio Grande

PAGE 24:
1. c
2. b
3. c
4. b
5. c
6. a
7. a
8. c

PAGE 26:
1. mountain, hill, plateau
2. canyon, valley
3. Both are low land. A valley doesn't have as high, steep walls as a canyon, and it isn't as narrow as a canyon.

PAGE 27:
1. It is more sheltered; the water might be calmer.
2. Both are partially enclosed by land.
3. peninsula
4. An island is completely surrounded by water while a peninsula is surrounded except for one side.
5. An island is surrounded by water. A lake is surrounded by land.

PAGE 28:
1. valley
2. red
3. plateau
4. Mississippi River
5. east and south

PAGE 29:
1. north
2. Kodiak
3. Alaska Peninsula
4. mountains
5. Yukon

PAGE 30:
1. People use them to make things.
2. roads, sandboxes, concrete
3. because natural gas burns

PAGE 31:
1. true
2. true
3. false
4. false
5. true
6. true

PAGES 32–33:
1. 38 to 40 inches of rain a year
2. north and west
3. 40 to 44
4. Houlton
5. Lewiston
6. greater
7. less than 38

PAGES 34–35:
1. northwest
2. Missouri River
3. Fort Laramie
4. Rocky Mountains
5. Snake River
6. The trail followed rivers and valleys.
7. The weather was better during spring and summer.
Word scramble: Oregon, Idaho, Nebraska, Kansas

PAGES 36–37:
1. picnic area
2. southwest
3. Take Kinney Road to Bajada Loop heading northeast. Go right onto Golden Gate Road. Then turn left on Picture Rocks Road.
4. Saguaro cacti
5. waterhole; to drink
6. Sandario Road

PAGES 38–39:
1. Hudson River; East River
2. east to west
3. north to south
4. southern
5. 59th Street; Fifth Avenue and Central Park West
6. Fifth Avenue and 42nd Street
7. east
8. west
9. It is easier to find places.

PAGES 40-41:
1. Fremont-Daly City Route
2. blue
3. Concord-Daly City
4. yes
5. Concord, Daly City, Richmond, Fremont
6. It's a transfer stop where people can change trains.
7. Richmond-Fremont
8. northeast
9. San Francisco Bay
10. over bridges, by boat, by plane

PAGE 42:
1. 5 to 10 inches of rain
2. coasts
3. 10 to 20 inches
4. less than 5 inches a year
5. Canberra
6. Indian, Pacific
7. southeast
8. All are true.

PAGE 43:
1. Map 1
2. 200
3. 10
4. Sacramento
5. 500
6. Pacific Ocean
7. Nevada, Arizona
8. national border

PAGE 44:

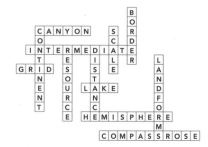